OFF WHITE
OFF WHITE
OFF WHITE
OFF WHITE

OFF WHITE

OFF WHITE

OFF WHITE

· annie bryan ·

I love you! Thank you for being so enthusiastic + supportive. I hope you enjoy it.

Love always,
Annie

OFF WHITE

{ a collection of autobiographical lyric essays on coping with coming out, eating disorders, anxiety, family trauma, adolescence and destruction in Suburbia Americana and other things that sting }

by annie bryan

copyright © annie bryan 2017. all rights reserved.

write hard and clear about what hurts.
-- hemingway

Printed 2017 by Broken Column Press
BrokenColumnPress.com
ISBN: 978-1-944616-15-1

not "to"
or "for"
but *with* you, B.

(here in your hands lies

my heart, my brain, my thoughts, my fears

no more than 100 short pages of admitting it all and all i've got

i hope you see yourself in one or all or all but one.

maybe you see yourself in none

so maybe you just listen, and for that i really ought to thank you.

thank you for seeing all of me. i owe you *e v e r y e v e r y t h i n g*.)

Table of Contents:

Gay   -   1-40

Skinny   -   41-56

Broken   -   57-82

Annie Bryan

i.

GAY

Off White

"experiment"

it's ok if you think twice.
i'm telling you as someone who has
been There
that not only it gets better
but you could and should and have and WILL question it.

i'm telling you as someone who has been There
that you are worth so much more than your first boyfriends made you think
and that you are going to be so much better than any of them ever measured you up to be
and that you will be EVEN BETTER because they didn't think so!

i am here to tell you that you will enjoy it for once,
yeah, you know. *it.*
you will enjoy it without gagging or crying or sweating or dreading
or waiting for the end to come,
because for once it will be about you.

i'm here to tell you that you deserve it,
to remind you that it's your turn to be happy,
to encourage you to embrace it when someone sheds light on you
(and just you).

i love you and you love yourself,
starting today.

soon enough we became careful nomads.   collectors of nothing in particular.   *obsessed* with the crevices of each other's cores when all our words became oceans that filled in all the gaps of each other's globes.   i forget what my map even *looked* like without the blue space all filled in and thank god for that.   you will always be my favorite continent.

so it's not that i got jealous as much as it is that i get more and more certain.   of beauty of intention of symmetry.   sometimes i ask too much and maybe even make you think the fear is bigger than the certainty which is not true.   it's that maximizing the blue makes the green more worthwhile so i crave the blue all the time. i can't stop nor do i want to.

I guess this is all to say that very simply the currents of your serotonin make my globe stop and my insides turn instead and i like that.

Annie Bryan

I remember what it felt like to think about how that one little breakfast felt so big because
we had never had a meal together before

I remember realizing that we had never had one on one time
Or the opportunity to talk too personally
I remember being so excited for that.

I remember thinking that my one chance to be with you had passed
That I'd never have the opportunity to tell you how i felt again,
RIP

I remember thinking that
We had never had breakfast together.
We had never had lunch together.
We had never cuddled together.
We had never cuddled together in *my* bed.

We had never watched a movie together.
We had never watched your *favorite* movie together.
We had never watched the stars together.
We had never watched each other together.

I don't remember a time when i wasn't imagining what all of those would feel like.
I don't remember a time when images of all those firsts *weren't* swirling around my head.

I remember you thinking i was straight, and i remember me thinking you were taken.

I remember thinking you were exceptionally out of my league. i still do.

I remember thinking that i needed to start shaving again
or maybe girls don't care about that kind of thing?

Off White

I don't remember thinking that you might actually finally be interested, too.
I imagine that was a good feeling.

I don't remember missing any of my exes. i imagine, for the first time, i didn't.

I remember hoping we'd still be together by your birthday because i wanted an excuse to do something special without you feeling self-conscious about it.

I remember admitting to myself that i liked you in October. i remember admitting to you that i liked you in December.

I remember knowing i was going to love you in February.
I don't remember realizing that i actually did. i imagine that happened in April.

I remember thinking that if i was going to be with you then i needed to stop
drinking too much
and eating too little
and thinking too much
and loving myself too little
and letting my laundry pile up because even though you wouldn't judge,
you'd never let your own pile get too big.

I don't remember bringing you Cheez-Its and chocolate. You do, though.
I don't remember telling you that one stupid story about my favorite writer's childhood that i read in some magazine last summer. You do, though.

I remember when you told me how that song reminds you of me, too.

I remember you telling your best friend
I remember you telling me you told your best friend

Annie Bryan

I remember being surprised, excited, nervous, proud, certain.

I remember thinking you were far too deliberate to do this without knowing the consequences
And i remember realizing that you believed we had a real shot.
I remember wondering why.

I remember you telling me how terrified you'd been to meet your exes' parents, how much you dreaded it, how strongly you tried to persuade them that you shouldn't.
I don't remember how i asked you to meet my mom.

I remember a year before i met you when i couldn't wait for summer so i could go home already.
I imagine spring coming and i get sad. Spring means summer and summer means you're leaving.

I remember you getting the job in India!
I remember being ecstatic for you, i remember you being ecstatic for yourself.
I remember you being terrified for me.

I remember thinking that if only my closed-minded family could meet you
that they would finally understand, they'd have to understand, how could anyone not understand
after standing in your light and witnessing your warmth. You are so warm.

I remember visibly shaking because i was so nervous and i remembering you offering me a sweatshirt.
I don't remember the frigid walk home. i know i wasn't nervous anymore.

I remember wanting to deserve you. i still do.

seven

we were collectors of nothing in particular.

senators of the ordinarily spontaneous.

berlin was very pointy but

the colors of venice looked good on you.

Annie Bryan

warmth.

your eyes look like coming home and *endearing* you are so endearing

and i've never felt as fuzzy as i did during christmastime when i was little
when santa was real and nothing was impossible if you asked him nicely enough
and it wasn't so hard to get up and go to school with the fuzzies deep in your chest

but i feel that fuzzy now and it's not so hard to get up anymore
it was so hard to get up for so long but now it's not because i look forward to you like i looked forward to santa

and i used to get scared when i went to school and had a deep sense of dread and anxiety
over nothing even though i knew i had nothing to fear.
it only went away when i had things to focus on, like school and books and christmas
and i started feeling that dread again when i got to college,
but you pulled me out of it.
and you gave me something to look forward to and something to keep me going and something to make me feel special and worthwhile and *good* inside
i haven't felt this warm and calm and *good* inside in so long.

my friend said that when he fell in love with a boy for the first time
that the whole world finally felt
like it was just the right size.

everything feels like it's been squeezing and trying and pulling and forcing it to fit for so long
and like it finally fits and im not trying anymore

you're a girl and i like you and it's *ok*
and i can say that and that's *ok*
and i'm *OK*
and everything is ok!

Off White

you are so warm that you got me unstuck
and the world is just the right size.

throwing up feelings & words & the food i couldn't even swallow
because i was so excited to see you again

they say that happens to your body when you're in love. they say
your pupils dilate too and i look you in the eyes a lot because it's
the most vulnerable sight i think i've ever seen. they're so freaking
blue and big but
do you look at everybody like that?

i've been simultaneously falling in love with you and grieving
losing you since i met you
but once in a while i think that just *maybe*

you could go far away and we could stay together and then maybe
i'll go far away too
because we've always talked about getting out of here and i'm so
glad you finally are
and god i wish i were too

you could go far away and we could stay together because we stick
together here to stay warm.
you know maybe we can end up together somewhere where we
don't even need to create our own warmth
did you ever think about that?

i've thought about it a lot. i hope we get unstuck somewhere warm
some day.

Preamble: May.

Hey, do you ever think about all the things you have yet to do? Me too! Yeah! Exactly! It's like when you feel as if you've finally seen what you've been waiting to see or do what you've been waiting to do and got to the place you always wanted to get to and you realize you have so many more places to see just like this one and faces to see just like yours and man i'm glad we met. Right? Totally, things always come together in the weirdest ways. And i wanna ski and surf and see stars and start living, like really *living*, you know? For sure. Haha i'm so glad you get it. That's incredible! Wish I'd been there. That makes a lot of sense to me. Seriously, it does! Everything makes sense right now. No thank YOU! Of course, any time. i love talking to you, too. i feel like I've known you a long time. i'm glad i stayed over, too.

Postamble: September.

Hey, yeah, now works! Tell me everything. That's incredible! i wish i was there, too. i miss you, too. i get it. i really get it. i wish things could be different. It doesn't make sense right now—nothing makes sense right now—but i'm sure one day it will, ok? Of course i remember— we had just started out but i felt like I'd known you forever. Me too, it's been a long time but i still totally feel like we just started out! But God i haven't seen you in forever. Oh, no worries— i'll talk to you later, ok? No yeah, for sure. Anytime. i love talking to you, you know that. i love you and i'm glad we stayed together, too.

Significant Hesitations: A love story

I think she's cute. Just blatantly, simply beautiful. i wouldn't tell her that. Much too forward.

She's so nice! i think i like her. Even more attractive as i get to know her little mannerisms. i won't tell her that. It probably isn't mutual.

I can't believe it's mutual. i think we should date. i probably won't ask though-- could be bad timing for her.

I can't believe we are dating. This is going so well. i think we should stay together. i won't tell her that – i don't want to pressure her.

I think she's perfect. For me and for everyone and all by herself. i'll probably never tell her that. She would think i didn't mean it.

When i told her she was perfect she choked up and i can't even say how sweet it was. How glossy her perfect blue eyes got. i thought to myself that i love her. i could never tell her that, i don't think she feels it as much as i do. Don't want to make her stress out about it. She's got enough on her plate as it is.

I told her i love her. i told her not to say it back.

She said it back.

  i'll never stop saying it.

Off White

I just remember leaning to put my head on your chest and realizing the window was wide open and thinking about the stupid frat boys probably watching us and i didn't give a damn. It was freeing.

It was snowing and the sky was navy and coral-y pink and the city lights were flickering and you looked as flawless as you always do – the girl with the bright blue eyes and wild curly blond hair whose birthday's in April was smiling up at me. If anything, i hoped somebody else got to witness it so i wouldn't be the only one who knew it really happened.

It was hard to keep kissing you when i was smiling too much because i was thinking about how long I've liked you and how much i wanted to tell you that and how much better i feel with you than with those guys. It was hard not to smile thinking about them seeing me with you now:

sparkling and melting and exhaling, still and full and calm and bright.

Annie Bryan

Death Cab for Cutie as The Eucharist

They never told me in Church that i might be the one to go to Hell.

As they warned me of those that fall into the Devil's traps, that end up in the Fiery Pits,

As the priest dressed me in my alter robes he never mentioned that

I could fuck up →   I could be one of The Sinners.

The Nuns forgot to say that God's Everlasting Love and Pearly Gates were for the Best Fit only

That my contract with The Lord & The Church is up as soon as i kiss a girl

You say i'm confused & rebellious, i'm just in a phase… & am i sure that i'm… you know. ?

You're right: I am confused.

 i'm confused b/c Mr. Schapiro + Mr. Tomlinson ≠ *1 Timothy 6:10*

& b/c the old ladies with giant pearls dangling from their ears ≠ *Leviticus 19:28*.

(I had to memorize that one.)

Off White

Does God hate that i kissed a girl on Sat. > that i pretend sick to skip church twice/month?

i'm just trying to make some God damn sense of these rules

b/c honestly, Father Pat, i'm not following your logic.

They never told me in church that i might be the one to go to hell.

colors

baby pink. wrinkly and twisted in an "O" to look as tiny as she feels. she purses her lips when she's sad. she's got bright blue eyes that get brighter and bluer and glossier and bigger when she cries. the outsides get a little pink from crying, too. baby pink like her pursed lips.

people tell her a lot that she reminds them of someone—a sister, an actress, a long lost childhood best friend they wish they hadn't lost touch with. the way they imagine their favorite character from a book. imperfect. uncompromising. beautiful.

pesky hair

there's this one hair on her head that always sticks up. actually, all of her hairs stick up—her curls are wild and bouncy and platinum blonde, naturally. she hates them. like any good lovable, quirky, protagonist that doesn't know her own worth— she hates them. especially the one that sticks straight up. it's imperfect. uncompromising. beautiful.

sula

when we talked for the first time about her graduating— really talked about it—we were sitting on her bed, across from a chipotle bag taped to her wall as décor. she liked the quote it had printed on it. she loves good quotes.

she grabbed a hardback book with tinted golden pages and tiny, perfectly neat blue ink penmanship written in it. sula, by toni morrison. all of morrison's books are about grief and dealing with love and hardship, usually at the same time. she opened it up and flipped through the first few pages to show me the opening epigraph quote and passed it to me as she sat back down. she leaned her head on my shoulder—with her bright blond hair sticking up and brushing my neck—and cupped her mouth. i didn't notice she had started to cry until after i read it aloud.

"it is sheer good fortune to miss somebody long before they leave you."

Off White

what you have heard is not true. it's nothing you expected and she is completely in control. a hole in the wall that is the **least like a ceiling**, the **most like a thunderstorm.** in a silent neon sky. she moves with you *lower* and *deeper* and *swiftly* and *deliberately* until you are both submerged. **she stops and says she does not remember the way** but you're certain she does. hesitate and continue; it should be downhill from here. you are **simultaneously drowning in cold water and completely on fire**, and you are surprised that it does not hurt. it tingles and it takes away all other senses. **in the billiards room with a candlestick and no hands.** she didn't admit it then but it was a different time. you will take the blame for her now. around the long table are all the people she used to know, sliced the most cleanly, and purposefully distanced from. looking at you like **they remember exactly what irked you**. which parts still sting. but there are conditions: you are not to move any lower and you must get out fast, never to mention this again. ***it happened exactly as she expected.***

Annie Bryan

this spot is free

somehow everyone already knows i kissed a girl last saturday

and for some reason it matters so much this time
because even though all those girls kiss each other too
they do it in front of the frat guys at the house parties after they
take body shots off each other
so it's different

they said it's different because i kissed her in the dark and i kissed
her when it was just us and i kissed her without all the stupid boys
stupidly cheering us on.

and now i kind of want to crawl in a hole and pretend it didn't
happen
even though it made me understand why all my girl friends do
such drastic things for the boys they like.

and why they talk about their hook ups so much as if they were the
best things that have ever happened to them
because this was easily one of the best things to ever happen to me
and i just wanna talk to everyone about it the way that they wanna
talk to everyone about the time the football player kissed them
but i don't wanna talk to them about it in the way they're talking
about it
the he-said she-said   she-kissed   she-kissed-back kind of
talking about it

and today i made a pretend list of "people to interview" because i
wanted to write your name
and i didn't want anyone to make fun of me for liking you

but this place is so isolating and
endearing, you are so endearing
i cant quite find the right words but

stunning. you are so stunning

Off White

and i'm sorry that i tried to convince them that i meant nothing
and i'm sorry i didn't text you the next day — i didn't forget. i wanted to.
and i'm sorry i looked at you a little too long in class, i didn't mean to do the thing the stupid boys do when they stare too much for too long like they deserve it
i don't deserve it
but god you are so stunning.

i couldn't look away, i tried to,

and now you're sitting next to the pretty girl in class with the big blown out hair
who doesn't even like girls but she knows that you'll compliment her if she fishes enough
so you do and she smiles but she might as well have said those reassuring words in the mirror
and you might as well have said them through gritted teeth.
she's one of the ones that made fun of me for kissing you that night.

come sit by me next time.

Annie Bryan

3rd wheel

first, heartbreaking.

thinking that changing the settings of my dating apps
to check off both the "women and men" boxes
might be liberating, affirming.
maybe checking different boxes would even eliminate the necessity
to explain my identity
because every god damn time it comes up in conversation it's a
maze to prove that i'm sure.

only to be invited again, and again,
and *again*
to be a fun fling between you and your boyfriend
who just want to add a little third wheel to the picture, no strings
attached,
but if i'm bi now so i guess i can't blame them for assuming?

then, infuriating

as if my sexuality is for your pleasure
as if i have any intention to seek your attention by now

as if it's kinky-cool-erotic and not just *normal*
a characteristic that took me 19 years to dub it

do you think it's hot that i cried myself to sleep the night before
my catholic confirmation
because i was scared of liking a girl and going to hell and being a
Bad Person

does it turn you on that i hated my butt that you and Stupid Boy
friends gawked at so much that i starved myself to make it go
away?

coming out has been so painful and difficult and confusing
and mentally and emotionally draining and impossible
so i'm glad someone's benefitting from this.

Off White

I went on a date today.

It went terribly. Know why? Because she was perfect. Seriously—it was great and i'm certain i like women, she was lovely and the food was lovely and i felt comfortable and engaged and

I talked about you.

I didn't think twice
Until i realized I'd brought you up—
talked at length, with a stranger,
twice.

3 glasses of wine later and 2 subway stops from home
i wondered why I didn't feel bothered
at the idea that there might not be more than 1 date

Wondered if that means i'm not really gay
She's smart and she's passionate and she's funny and she's laid back
And she's caring and she's calm and she's humble and she's beautiful and she's sexy
"but she's not ___"

I can't find the courage to write it down, but last night on the one,
With strangers around me after a date with a stranger,
I said it aloud.

It's kind of fun to admit things out loud.

What happened last night?

B: Well she stayed until 5:30 am and we just talked and talked and had this great conversation and didn't realize so much time had passed and i don't know man, i don't know if she likes me?

A: Yeah i stayed until just a couple of hours before i had to get up—of course i didn't tell her that, are you kidding? Yeah but i'm just not sure if she sees me that way because we could also just be friends

Do you think you'll call her?

B: Of course not. i couldn't do that, you know me. i'm not like that. Way too much pressure. I'd rather she just made the first move.

A: Of course not. She's not like that. Plus i don't want to pressure her, she'd feel bad and pressured and i don't want to do that.

Do you like her?

A: i have. For 6 months, and very much.

Do you think anything will happen?

A: i mean, i didn't used to have a shot. i might now. i might not take it. Should i take it? Probably not.

B: Probably not. Not unless she made a move. Timing's terrible anyway.

Do you want anything to happen?

A, B: Of course.

Annie Bryan

She made me curious about the world
And i made her want to settle down for the first time
(maybe even close to mom & dad).

She felt like a Thursday early evening with a chilly sun
And an orange sky with a drink in hand on the back porch.
Always has.

I worry i might feel like a Sunday late afternoon
When you know you've got a lot to do
And everything's going to be fine this week
Because you ARE ready
And she says you DO matter
But you don't **feel** ready
And things are just right but maybe too right to be determined

But she says "few things make me happier than a blue sky with white clouds"
And she looks at me like i'm one of them.

And it all felt like a river that was heading towards the sea
Though we did not know which one

And so i go on loving you
        Percussively
Like water.

Off White

Blossoming

I've always had it in me
I was just sculpting
& creating
& reaping the womanly
goodness and power
that's been bubbling up in me

I almost lost it but i discovered it again. Don't worry.
You have a sparkle too
And one day you'll get out of there
And they'll say they always saw it in you
And you'll smile
They'll fall to their knees and they'll fall to their sameness

Trust me.
Bow down

Sticky

This could go one of a few ways:

***

Most likely, you get a job far away in a place that's warm like you
and i get stuck here
and you decide that it's probably healthiest for yourself and for me that we go our separate ways
And you say that you're not what's best for me right now.
You always think about what's healthiest and what's best for me. That's what i'll miss most.
and i'm happy for you and suck it up because didn't i go into it knowing it would probably have to end this way anyway?

***

Less likely, you get a job far away
In a place that's warm like you and i stay stuck here
And you decide that I've been there for you and that this is worth a shot
But eventually you need to focus on your work and your friends and your new life because
I was really just around while you still felt attached to this place but now you're in that place
And that place has so much to offer you, more than i have to offer you,
because all i have to offer you is memories and comfort and you don't need those anymore.

You're so afraid of getting stuck. You don't want to stop learning and growing and challenging.
i'm so afraid of losing you. You called it a sticky situation. i don't want to be the sticky place you get stuck in.
i'm afraid of being stuck here while you're getting unstuck.

I know how afraid you are of getting stuck.

Off White

***

Least likely,
You get a job and a home in a place that's warm but you say what's warmest and homest is me
And that of course i'm not holding you back
and that along with the memories and the comfort there's so much that i teach you too,
you've always said this isn't a one-way street when i thought it might be
And you become a world traveler and give it 1 maybe 2 years and i'm travelling too and neither of us is stuck and both of us are growing
And the comfort and the memories and the unstuck and the learning and growing and challenging are all there and neither of us is giving up anything and both of us are gaining everything
And we've got so much and so much on the line but lose nothing because we hoped   we planned   we *knew* we just knew it would be this way
it just *had* to be this way if anything was going to make sense

My friends say i need to calm down. "you haven't even kissed the girl yet!" "time will tell."
You told them that you won't hurt me, that you've been thinking about it a lot.

And it's not like i could suppress my feelings if i wanted to
Because as soon as i told you how i felt the snowball was rolling and growing just like you rolling out of here and growing out of me
and I've been feeling like im constantly on the verge of throwing up since October
Throwing up feelings & words & the food i couldn't even swallow because i was so excited to see you again

They say that happens to your body when you're in love and your pupils dilate too and i look you in the eyes a lot because it's the most vulnerable sight i think i've ever seen and they're so freaking blue and big but do you look at everybody like that?

I've been simultaneously falling in love with you and grieving losing you since i met you
But once in a while i think that just *maybe*

You could go far away and we could stay together and then maybe i'll go far away too
because we've always talked about getting out of here and i'm so glad you're finally getting out of here
and god i wish i were too
You could go far away and we could stay together because we stick together here to stay warm
You know maybe we can end up together somewhere where we don't even need to create our own warmth
did you ever think about that?

I've thought about it a lot. i hope we get unstuck somewhere warm someday.

LDR

it's not as hard as it used to be you know because it's not that i miss you just a little bit all the time anymore it's that i miss you a whole lot every once in a while when i see something and think "she would love this" and "i wish i could show her this" because there's so much that makes me think "i wish i could show her this" so the Net Missing You is probably lower than it used to be. but then again i guess slightly-missing-you-all-the-time moments have turned into missing-you-a-ton-all-at-once but i think that also means i still miss you all the time it's just subconscious now so i guess it's more painful now than it used to be. i guess it's just as hard as it used to be, i've just gotten used to it.

Annie Bryan

You know I've tried to send my friends pictures of you to give them an idea about what your aura is like and i know it sounds cliché but god photos just don't do it justice
I wish i could show them the way you looked at me right after we kissed for the first time
Embarrassed and calm and happy and like everything we'd both been stressing out about was finally past and god you were so happy
It felt exactly like i imagined it was going to and you're everything i imagined you were going to be and i think to myself all the time that i'm just so fucking lucky
And you looked up at me like i was the most nurturing loving healing thing you'd ever seen, i never noticed you look at me like that before
And you looked so small you looked like you could just break
I never saw you look like that before.

I said something sweet that i really meant but you thought it was ridiculous
And you threw your head back and let out the deepest realest laugh

and god the way you looked at me i wish i could show them
I wish i could give everyone someone that looks at them the way you looked at me
You just looked so happy and so free and like such a *girl*
and it didn't matter to me
actually, i liked it.

and god kissing you was like when the hot water first kicks in in the shower and all your muscles finally *relax* everything just clicked and felt right and when you pulled back and hugged me and i swear everything deflated.

Off White

My teacher told me not to use hearts in poem metaphors.

But i don't mean a conceptual heart,
Not a "Give you my heart" kind of heart
Love. Kindness and all that

I mean a human heart:

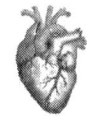

🫀 , not ❤.

I mean i need you,
I mean you are what makes me conscious

You are real and consistent in rhythm
And human and flawed and vulnerable but don't you see

I mean without you i have functioning parts but cannot feel whole, alive.

You are my heart.

i.

The trouble with this situation in particular is that i know what it
feels like for someone you think is your friend and *just* your friend
to admit that they had different intentions all along
And you know that this whole time your friendship was still real
but was it really?
And it doesn't feel good and you know you should be flattered but
you feel a little bit used you feel a little bit like
The time that the washrag frayed so much from face masks that it
came undone completely and we threw the string and the bubbles
at each other and laughed and laughed and everything came
undone and the world was just the right size

So now i'm sitting next to you and everything is fine because
everything is always fine with you
But everything hurts and nothing is fine because this will always be
a secret, it has to be a secret, i promise i'll keep it a secret.

Even though nothing fits together quite right
And the world is not the right size.

ii.

If you ever read this (I really hope you do and God i really hope
you don't) i'm sorry that i couldn't keep it a secret anymore.

iii.

sometimes i think about how we used to talk about how we
weren't sure why or boyfriends took our relationships so seriously
why they always told us they wanted to be our Forever, we thought
it was crazy.
About when we both came out to ourselves and to each other we
looked back at that and them
and we laughed and laughed.
how silly they were to think we were their Forever

Just a thought

Off White

do you ever think we are forever?

iv.

I mean come ON i know you're happy and that makes me happy
but it's not like she's anything close to your match
I mean i know i'm biased but it's not like she gets all your jokes
and quirks and smirks and all the little things
You haven't been together that long, i know that
but i got it all right away, you know that
Sometimes i think about the way that *every* time a girl likes you, you tell me you're not as into it as she is
And you tell me about how you are sort of just going along with the relationship
and it's kinda funny to admit out loud but you feel bad about not feeling more

it's kind of fun to admit things out loud.

but you're just not feeling it because you don't usually feel a whole lot
And you really do feel bad for the poor girl, even though it sounds ridiculous so we laugh and laugh and laugh

But i'm your best friend and we are each other's whole worlds and
we feel every everything for each other
so would you, could you
be as into it as i am?

I tell you not to feel bad because you don't feel it as much as she does.

If you don't feel it as much as i do don't feel bad
But please just let me know – I've got to know
do you feel anything at all?

v.

this place is cold and sometimes all i want is a little extra of you
because you're what makes it homey
so sometimes when i think of our friendship and how great it is
and what "more" would look like
and how much more "more" could be
homesick, i get homesick.

sometimes i look at what you and your girlfriend have and God i just *know* we could be a little more.

sometimes i look at what you and your girlfriend have and i miss it.

Is it possible to be homesick of a place you've never been before?

vi.

your smile takes me home and this place is always cold
sometimes too cold
and my God it hurts when you're all out of breath and the wind whips you in the face
and the blood on your lips tastes like copper

if i found a penny face-up I'd give it to you, shiny or not.

vii.

You know me very well so i can't help but think that you've got to know by now you've got to have a clue that i don't just want to be friends now and always

You've got to know that i didn't whip out my laptop and start typing like my fingers were on fire when you took me back to your girlfriend's room just because i had an email to write
As we all sat there to get work done like 3 normal friends but you sat next to me instead of next to her and you had to know that it wasn't normal and i could never feel normal because

Off White

You're cracking jokes that she doesn't get because we have so many inside jokes
And i feel bad that she feels left out but god it's not possible to act like this is normal it's not normal that we have this much chemistry, more than you'll ever have with her and it's not just a matter of time until she'll get you like i do
And it's not just a matter of time until we get together. it very possibly might just never happen.

You've got to know that everything is on fire and i want to

viii.

burn i want to burn i want to light myself on fire in moments like these because at least that would be feeling something because right now i'm numb from inaction and i'm numb from feeling everything and saying nothing

ix.

if you ever read this, i'm not sorry. It will always be this way.

x.

sometimes i think long and soft about what we could have and i miss it

Annie Bryan

These pages are for you. Write something.

Off White

Annie Bryan

Off White

ii.

SKINNY

Off White

ED Test

follow this in order, answer honestly
and press enter to continue
because you don't know until you know
and you don't have to be skinny to have an eating disorder.

when you eat   but only 3 grapes an hour
and love your body   but only after you peed or skipped a meal
and you have "fitness goals"   but only to look like all the other
girls that have acted even more drastically on their insecurities

they're not just insecurities
they're eating disorders.

and it's ok to ask for help.

Off White

Stretched
THIN

(145)

Not hungry
Want food
Don't eat!
Pick nails

So bored
Want comfort
Don't eat!
Count calories

Thin already
Hair falling
Clothes looser
Skin looser

Good feedback
Feeling better
"You look great!"
Thank you.

(135)

People notice!
Validation,
Finally.
Need more

Juice cleanse
New fad
Diet pills
Firming cream

Meal time
Past max
Don't eat!
"What's wrong?"

(125)

Supplements
Thinspiration
Track exercise
Log food

So hungry
Want food
Nervous stomach
Can't swallow

And losing
And shrinking
And succeeding
At last!

"so skinny!"
don't tell
"get help!"
can't backtrack

(120)

not hungry
used to it
eyes sunken
bad temper

lost a pound
lost a pant size
lost a cup size
lost control
lost a friend
lost hair
lost respect
lost my mind

(115)

not hungry
not healthy
"you look sick"
thank you.

when i ate carbs i looked in the mirror and felt disgusting
so thank god i'm over that
right?
i mean i'm so much happier now and that what counts
my therapist said that's what counts

when i was fat boys grabbed my ass and it made me think
they were making fun of me
so thank god there's nothing to grab anymore
i made sure there's nothing to grab anymore

now that i'm tiny my whole body shakes when my stomach grumbles
suddenly needing a snack is earth shattering.
i hope no one notices

and today i didn't eat until my stomach hurt
then i ate until my stomach hurt
then i threw up until my throat hurt
then i cried because everything hurt
and i cried until nothing hurt and everything just got numb.

i'm so much happier skinny

"Got a towel, dear?"

It's hard not to COMPLETELY lose your shit when you walk into the kitchen – " i'm home" – to see your aunt surrounded by a pool of blood,

after "accidentally" slicing open her thigh – her pale, frail, knobby thigh – again and again leaving gashes like crevices between tectonic plates,

so torn apart you can't imagine them closing up again, so deep that they don't look right on her limp limb, on the first Saturday of winter –

she could never handle the cold or the dimness, or even just the cheerful carolers and fake santas and jingles that she couldn't relate to –

while "cooking pasta" that she absolutely did not need the steak knife for – "vegetarian" because she doesn't eat so "excuse her small stature" –

barefoot on the cold hard tile by the cold hard granite counter speckled with some of the last few drops of warm liquid life she had in her

The day i told my mom i had an eating disorder was the day i disappointed her most. It wasn't because she blamed me, or because she thought i couldn't handle it, or because she thought i was in physical danger. She just wished she had known sooner. She wished she'd noticed it in me sooner. She wished her parents had noticed it in her sisters sooner.

I was 20 years-and-1-trainwreck old when i made the phone call. It was my grandfather's 86th birthday.

***

She said that she never talked to me about it because she didn't even want to entertain the conversation, afraid of legitimizing my misconstrued and horribly negative body image.

***

One day when i was 15, i asked my mom is she thought i was fat. She flipped a shit.

I remember thinking it was strange because i'd asked her many times before if she thought i was fat and she never had much of anything to say about it. i wondered why this time in particular struck such a chord.

I never asked her again.

***

When i was 17, my mom caught me throwing up a Fiber One brownie in her bathroom before taking my post-workout shower.

She asked me what was wrong. i said i felt ill.
She told me to take a nap.
I did it many times after that.

Off White

Grandma's Kitchen

Ceramic is quaint until it slices open a vein. Delicate green vases line the shelves, as crisply as you did your lines off the counter, through the glass paneled case that displays everything prideful except for the repurposed jars full of snow white coke fairy-dust and cinnamon.
(Drugs take you elsewhere, spices suppress appetite.)

There is a photo of grandpa gardening with the lady he used to visit
in New York. Framed out of spite, i'm sure.
A few dates never killed anybody until it actually did.

Lisa comes into the kitchen after a nap and a coffee,
looking like she hasn't had either but "don't *you* ever leave the house?"
Looks at the photo of grandpa, says he needs a visitor once in a while,
Has no intention of that person being her.
She looks smaller than usual in an XL sweatshirt
(and we both know she did that on purpose.)

I say i'll head out in a bit
and immediately think of all the places i'll go instead.
"Thanks, you're a doll. Always been the favorite anyway."

A porcelain doll comes crashing down from the top shelf,
Bursting as it hits the hardwood
leaving specs of dainty ceramic fairydust
(and bigger shards that could slice open a vein just like THAT)
sprinkled all over the floor.

Annie Bryan

Cinnamon

Because the only thing you left behind for me was a

Cabinet full of cinnamon,
Sugar-free gum, a staged living room—now full of death
And all these fucking pills

Prescriptions you saved from
Times you were sick
And times i was sick
And times grandma was sick
And times your patients were sick

And they'll say as we bury you along with all your secrets
That you overdosed on accident
A fluke tragedy, a brilliant woman.

And they'll say that it's a shame
Such a qualified nurse didn't know better

But i know better. i knew as soon as i heard you were missing.

"A mother to all, so sad that she was infertile"
    -- (infertile because she refused to eat)
"a caregiver at heart, she always loved nursing"
    -- (to steal pills she could abuse after work)

You're the reason she's a psych nurse
And the reason he's a neuroscientist
And the reason i'm a journalist
Because we are all so thirsty for the TRUTH finally

Off White

You never did and now you never will fork it up to me but i know i have it anyway,
And i refuse to inherit your lies

Rest in peace thinking that your secret is safe with me.
Rest in the peace that you never let me have

Annie Bryan

These pages are for you. Write something.

Off White

Annie Bryan

Off White

iii.

BROKEN

Off White

when we had no money my mom would make my dad write GRATITUDE at the top of his to-do list every day.   he writes in his franklin planner each morning and each night.   i think because it reminds him of when we did have money when he did have things he needed to do.   a working man.   whereas suddenly after the Bad Day he had nothing to do and everything to change about our lives.   i know he cried a few times but not very often.   i don't remember it much because it's not who he was or has been ever since.   the dog loves no one but man does my dog love my dad, he would sit next to my dad every day while he sat at his desk in the coldest darkest corner of the basement in the room that doesn't have any windows in a room that only exists otherwise as a storage closet.   at some point he shed the anxiety because my mom made him write GRATITUDE at the top of his reminders so even if he couldn't feel grateful he'd remember that he should. my dog loves no one but man does my mom love that dog, she usually can't deal with the thought of dogs because they remind her of her angry italian father who beat the hell out of her childhood labrador.   but our beagle was beaten and abandoned and so was my mom.   and somehow my mom is still grateful for those that got her out of there and she likes to think the dog just might be too.

Off White

I Don't Know It If Was Rape

Don't assume that what you heard is true because i promise if all you've heard is his side of it it's not true i swear it's not true

I wasn't as horrible as he makes me sound and i only snapped because he wanted me to snap
I wouldn't have said all that stuff if he hadn't done all that stuff
And i wouldn't have done all that stuff if he hadn't said all that stuff

i'm not a crazy slut and i didn't even have sex with that guy it was just one kiss one stupid kiss

And he was really nice to me actually but i thought we weren't gonna tell anyone
And we weren't even together so it's not like it was cheating
But it doesn't matter who it was or where it was or when it was or what the circumstances were
He's gonna make it sound like i started it

And its not even that i'm less dramatic or more mature but i don't know how to handle this so i guess i just wont i guess i just can't
Everyone already knows that i kissed him and everyone already hates me for it
(hates me in the loves-to-hate kind of way, the wants-to-hate so they feel a little better about themselves kind of way)

And i guess it was a warning when he told you he'll stay with you if you have sex with him
and you're "more likely not to break up"

and he hits you when you're getting intimate
even though you asked him not to
and grabs you that way you said made you feel bad
and calls you those names you said you didn't like

Does it count and who's to say and should i tell anybody?

Annie Bryan

How is it that you only do anything for me
When i'm asking nothing of you
And you can only give me the world
When i take myself out of yours?

In the words of my best friend's best friend
I will not sit and wait until your emotions are convenient for you.

I told you not to walk out of this house
But you told me not to walk out of your life
And look how well that went for you

I've found that all the poets are wrong
And
Love does not go with the seasons.

You know that i'm not into it unless
You too are too in it

To make it til next November
Then the holidays will carry us
through early spring

And spring comes with standstills like this all over again
But a warranty until then would be nice
I hope it's renewed in the season of new things
And we both know love's only fun when it's new so

we'll ruin it again
And again
Until it's new again

Isn't that how this always goes?

"Miss United States"

Don't trip. Don't frown. Tight tummy, don't breathe in too fast.
She's beauty and she's grace
Just to the end of the stage, pose sharp. Eye contact with camera.
She's queen of 50 states

All eyes on her. The kind of huge bugging eyeballs of a Green Whip Snake studying prey,
about to engulf it with its fangs, venom will stop every cell in a moment. Attack. Soon.

Same as watching NASCAR, or a satisfying trainwreck disaster. Hold your breath for contestants,
but hope their car runs into the side wall, bursts to flames. Makes for a better show.

A diamond is formed over time from careful, consistent, painstaking pressure from all sides
To be Perfect. Or else

She's elegance and taste, as long as she reins, as long as she wins…
unless she doesn't. In that case, deal's off, she is none of these things

Annie Bryan

Whiplash

Maybe it's cliché to call it whiplash

The "yo-yo" effect, or whatever,

But that's what it feels like.

And you don't know it until somebody, or something,

(Your *favorite* somebody, or something,)

Has turned on you.

It's like
When you're taking off a band aid
And you want to go slow, even though you know ripping it off would be easier
Because you *want* to feel the pain slowly

As if it numbs some other pain, makes you forget about some other worse stinging
Just for a moment
As you peel it from your skin
Clinging
Holding on
But then it's off of you, and it only takes a second
before your brain realizes the bigger pain is still there,
And it hits you again

It's like
when you're the top of the world, then something ever so briefly goes wrong,
And everything comes crashing down,
-- Or seems to, because one thing didn't go right, so the rest seems suddenly flawed too --
like when your favorite something is off for a moment
and the rest of your norms simply can't make up for it
and you feel like a failure, even though you were just doing so well,

Off White

because you fucked up that one little something,
the thing that didn't even seem to matter

It's most raw
When you're with someone
Who loves you, then doesn't,
Then does again,
Then didn't,
Always will // never did

But they *Loved* you, you *swear*
And you tell your friends they really did:
"She really didn't cheat before… it was just this one time."
"He didn't normally talk to me like that…"

Even though you really do remember that it wasn't all Bad,
until it was

And even though you know you're right--
It used to be so good, so warm, so easy--
And even if your friends aren't judging you,
It feels like they are
And it feels like you're stupid
You're the wrong one for getting carried away,
And you feel like you cheated yourself, like "you should've known better"

Another cliché that makes sense suddenly.
That you've always heard before, maybe even said before, but never related to,

Now you can.

Whiplash.

Ashes to Ashes

A new study analyzing bacterial communities involved in the decomposition of corpses illustrates how a cadaver becomes a living, thriving ecosystem for microorganisms.

When you die, your corpse will first turn greenish-
cafeteriavomityellow
Decomposition of the human body begins with flesh discoloration. Your dead self
will be a little damp to the touch, and you'll bloat a little.
Not your fault; that's just the bacteria

Don't worry, bloat will dissipate as bacteria eat your tissue: Inside out, intestines first

while your family and friends surround your tombstone
bacterial communities will be coming together, too,
moving through your guts, organ by organ.
Think of it like rinsing out your insides, with feces material. A trendy cleanse

Dressed to the nines and made up in a $3,000 coffin
the highest quality bed you'll ever rest in, looking better than you ever did alive.
At the edge of decease, one can sense velvet

triplet ivorydeath doves will be released, fly over the crowd in unison as practiced
Funeral processions in matching black cars (replicating bacterium migrating to the next organ)

Off White

"Got a towel, dear?"

It's hard not to COMPLETELY lose your shit when you walk into the kitchen – " i'm home" – to see your aunt surrounded by a pool of blood,

after "accidentally" slicing open her thigh – her pale, frail, knobby thigh – again and again leaving gashes like crevices between tectonic plates,

so torn apart you can't imagine them closing up again, so deep that they don't look right on her limp limb, on the first Saturday of winter –

she could never handle the cold or the dimness, or even just the cheerful carolers and fake santas and jingles that she couldn't relate to –

while "cooking pasta" that she absolutely did not need the steak knife for – "vegetarian" because she doesn't eat so "excuse her small stature" –

barefoot on the cold hard tile by the cold hard granite counter speckled with some of the last few drops of warm liquid life she had in her

Annie Bryan

Still-Life from Your Minivan's Rearview

Like the weeks after a distant relative's passing, aunt's-cousin-twice-removed who you MAYBE met once as a toddler,
Everyone wants to know what happened and how and Are you doing ok?

Everything *looks* different. Your future looks brighter with friends cheering you on,
It was good while it lasted // You're better off without him!
Painful but necessary, empowering but devastating, confusing and definite and relieving all at once.

Then everything stills. You're sitting at the kitchen table
          the table looks the same
The jars look the same, bed looks the same. The dopey dog looks dopey, plants are still potted
the mirror still reflects the ugly yellow-tinted hanging light fixture he always meant to replace

Overwhelming stillness   intermittent
vertigo. Heart, be not deceived...
Toothbrush, driveway, nightstand, heartbreak, carpet

Off White

Catholic guilt will kill you if you let it.
It killed both her sisters, but she wanted to break the cycle

17 when she left home for keeps,
The same age her mom had her first baby

A girl. A girl who would hold
The weight of the entire world—not a cliché, literally.
The weight of generations from across hemispheres
The weight from years upon years of bruises and dried up tears
that make the skin on your cheeks feel tight
Aunts and uncles and grandparents and cousins and *everyone*

Tight like that dress her first boyfriend told her to wear
And she did because all she's ever known is "ok."
"Ok, i will."   " i'm ok."   "Ok."

Tight like the only room she could afford in southwest Philly
Even tighter than the room she shared with her 2 sisters
With the same tears but tears but less bruises because she always took the fall for them when dad got mad after work or had a flashback to the war
Or when mom got violent on a bad trip from the drugs

The drugs that cost them all their money
That made the house so tight and the bruises so dark
The drugs that her sisters got to after she left for college
And turned into addictions that turned into stealing prescriptions from their patients
that turned into stealing prescriptions from their parents in hospice
what goes around comes around, i guess

God from god, light from light,
Blood from blood.
I don't think that's what they mean in church
But then again the first time he broke skin was in Sunday school.
That's what you get for talking back, i guess

The blood through him one in being with the father through him all things were made
The blood her mother showed her on a cotton pad in her panties saying, "this is what happens when you get leukemia"
Making up diseases to make her do all the housework
The blood her cousinfatheruncle drew fromherfromher arms legs wrists neck
from her head smashed against the refrigerator where she hung her own A+
from her private parts—she doesn't talk about that anymore.

Always reminded that obeying thy parents is in the bible and he always got angry when his bible pages folded after he threw it at her and it fell to the ground
That's what he/He wants after all, i guess

Off White

In Other News:

Society Investment, "Media Thing"
temperature of a story
community establishment thrown
in the Ofthepeople-bythepeople-forthepeople Oven
The ever-obvious difference in environment
of the rumor dealer,
advertising cigarette,
death of the customer

mood of the opinion and
blood of the audience
don't always mix well, this recipe
(resource agencies, flagrant promotion
college debt versus administration criticism)
preparation of a stage personality, usurping tradition
collapsed religion in all the election drama
Sector error--

--feedback excitement
outcome: permission to self-destruct; resolution: police satisfaction
Supermarket of the institutions,
reputation tales lining all sides
Potato requirements: seed, dirt, massive coverup plot!
Bad records obliterated
In the beginning models of profit
Culture egg shattered on the ice network countertop.

Steal my Sleep II

The fire alarm stopped going off
And the fire trucks drove away
And the firemen gave a wave and a thumbs up
But a fire is still fucking raging.
It's 5 am
And i have work at 8:30
And right now i'm wasting time giving you explanations to protect your feelings
Even though you never thought twice about mine

It's 5 am and i have work at 8:30
But i have never been more cognizant of the fact that i owe you
None of this
& more

Off White

every time i had a new boyfriend
i'd keep a note in my phone
and call it "conversations"
and fill it with all the sweet things they say

that way i'd have something to look back on
when i realized i could do better
but didn't have the energy to dump their sorry ass yet.

when i got around to ending it,
i'd delete the contents of the note,
and refill it with someone else's words later.

if you don't want to fill a girl's note--
her gaps,
her expectations, and her needs,
someone else will.

i promise.

Statistics

It happened to my mom when she was 19.
She was at her best friend Carol's beach house.
It was Carol's uncle.
He was 60. He had a wife. He had kids. She was studying to become a nurse, he said he would come over to let her get some practice using needles on patients. He was a diabetic.
He asked if he could take her shirt off, she felt paralyzed.
She didn't say it was assault. Actually, she didn't say anything. She still hasn't.

She was very sober. It was the middle of the day. She had to see him many more times after that.

It happened to me when i was 18.
He lived on my floor. He told me i owed it to him for flirting with him that night.
I was very sober. He pulled me into his lap, i scooted away. He pulled me back, he leaned in. His breath smelled like cheap malt liquor. i said i didn't want to. Then i said it again.
I felt weird about it. i didn't call it an assault.
I had to see him every day after that.

Until he was suspended for sexual assault after breaking into another girl's room. She lived down the hall as well.
Her lock was broken. He crawled into bed with her. She said it wasn't assault, he just didn't understand. Her roommate was worried, the RA found out what happened.
She felt bad when he was suspended. She felt guilty when she didn't see him after that.

It's hard to call it what it is when no one ever tells you what counts as sexual assault.

She was the 1 in 4.
My mom was the 1 in 4.
I am the 1 in 4.
Statistics don't lie. Society does.

The River is like The Subway and Sometimes A Door
(In that i like that i have the option to jump and i don't.)

I went down last night and thought about this and about how
rivers and their friends
divide cities in half. Especially in Europe, they always cut down the
middle.
They are unapologetic; they know we need their ports more than
they do.

I couldn't stop watching the flat masks peering over the footbridge
staring quizzically at the dark, inviting, rippling surface,
promising endings instead of offering reflections.

Urban spaces are funny this way. Rivers and subways and doors
Always lead somewhere new, there are few endings unless you
search for one.
Which many residents actually do-- hence the flat masks on
footbridge.

Because cities are overwhelming. Suffocating. Massive mazes that
are easy to get lost in.
So i can't help but see the irony in how subways and rivers break
them up
Into just barely digestible bits, breathable and navigable,
To help their dwellers survive. But they jump.

Or some do, i should say. Because when cities are overwhelming
And more people seem to be choosing to jump than not,
What keeps me from following along is that i have the option not
to. And i don't.

The Riddle

I am probably not all you remember me to be but i am better than you can find now.
It was purple and crumbly, but especially when the other blocks fell down
And i helped you hum all the right jingling notes inside our coziest blanket fort.

I can take you back to when there were frayed shoelaces
in loose bunny ears. Loops that did not whip.
Chain link fences that did not restrain – everything exciting was within.

What went wrong stayed between us. It wasn't a surprise.
We grew up and the bikes broke down and we forgot to ever change their tires.
Mom got old and Dad lost money, as soon as we were conscious enough to know.

Close your eyes. Imagine we are much older.
When all your clues are used up, is a guessing game fun anymore?

Off White

Three Days Back and One Foot Forward

Trimmed trees and tall grasses and tiny houses fly by
and i don't think the cows are moving.
You twirl, i blink and you're gone again.

The suit across the aisle critiques low-quality train merlot
and i just want to tell him how lucky he is to be with his "You"
Wrapped in a scarf with rectangular blue glasses like yours,
looking through them at him just like he's magic.

Outside it begins to rain. i brainstorm a list of how i could be worse off.
Cool girls that played soccer but looked like Barbie used to slam my forehead
and that stung so much more.

We stop next to a gas station that i bet sells
the stringy gum we liked to chew.
Imagine we never taste it again.
Imagine the train skips your dull yellow door
and i have to keep holding my breath

You told me once that you'd hijack the train, in that case
And make sure i got off safe and sound.
I sprint to the front car to make sure you're there

my mom is a psychiatric nurse.   my brother is a neuroscientist.   i've grown up hearing about the brain and talking about the brain and it's something that i should know a lot about by now.   but i don't.   i go to therapy and take medication for my anxiety and trust that it makes me feel better.   i believe that. i write about my feelings and talk about my mental health openly and am known for defending to the *death* every route of mental health care.   i believe in all of those as well.   but i don't know why my neurons don't fire quite right, what is going on that gives me those terrible panic attacks—   that keep me from breathing, that keep me from being able to stop shaking and blanking and freezing and sweating and heart-pounding.   i wish i knew why my brain doesn't work like everybody else's (except for those who do think like me, and for that and for them i am so sorry).   i wish i knew what kept me from being able to talk in class when i know i have a good point but just can't raise my hand.   or talk with my friends and family when i know there would be no repercussions and i know they would love to hear my voice, it's been so long since they heard my voice.   i miss it too.   (this is why i write). i wish i knew why getting out of bed is so hard but so is falling asleep.   and so is working out.   and so is doing homework. and so is calming down about knowing i have all of those things i need to do but can't.   i wish i knew which neurons were making laundry feel like such a task.   that make showering feel like a task. everything feels like a task but i can't do any of them because i feel paralyzed but also guilty, i feel guilty because i know i'm capable and responsible and liable but i just can't.   i wish i knew what was going on in my brain and why it doesn't always work quite right.

Off White

i imagine the pills you overdosed on were clear blue. tylenol pm. blue like the cerulean crayon— my favorite color in the 124-pack with the sharpener in the back that you gave peter and me for easter. blue like the shiny dress you wore to mom and dad's wedding, with your hair all curled and eyelashes all long and nails all perfectly shaped and polished. and such a light in your eyes. god you looked so different back then. i cherish those pictures. mom says they still sting too much.

blue like the color mom's eyes turn when she cries— they get bright and glossy blue. she cried so hard when she found out. i did, too. it was a tuesday after dinner and we were the only ones home and she was listening to me study history for my test the next day—mamabunny always pretended to "listen" when i "taught" her what i needed to learn when prepping for tests. we became best friends that year— you were her sister and i was her daughter but when you died so did Annie the Daughter. she just wanted a sister, you know. she always did.

blue like the school colors of the Dream College i got into—just like grandpa, everyone told me. you would've been so proud. i received my acceptance email with the "congratulations!" subject line exactly two months later, you know. two months to the day. you told me you couldn't imagine why anyone would turn me down. you made me think i could actually do it, you know.

i imagine the pills were blue like peter's bedroom fan— he got the blue one and i got the pink one because isn't that how it always went? you saw us so separately like that. i don't like pink anymore, you know. and i have a girlfriend now. her eyes are blue like mama's and peter's and yours.

you'd like her. she says i'm strong.
i always thought you were too, you know.

Write something. An ending. A reaction. A journal entry. Your grocery list.

Whatever it is, thank you for reading, and thank you for sharing in return.

Off White

Annie Bryan

Off White

Made in the USA
Middletown, DE
24 August 2017